Slender Warble

The Poiema Poetry Series

Poems are windows into worlds; windows into beauty, goodness, and truth; windows into understandings that won't twist themselves into tidy dogmatic statements; windows into experiences. We can do more than merely peer into such windows; with a little effort we can fling open the casements, and leap over the sills into the heart of these worlds. We are also led into familiar places of hurt, confusion, and disappointment, but we arrive in the poet's company. Poetry is a partnership between poet and reader, seeking together to gain something of value—to get at something important.

Ephesians 2:10 says, "We are God's workmanship . . ." *poiema* in Greek—the thing that has been made, the masterpiece, the poem. The Poiema Poetry Series presents the work of gifted poets who take Christian faith seriously, and demonstrate in whose image we have been made through their creativity and craftsmanship.

These poets are recent participants in the ancient tradition of David, Asaph, Isaiah, and John the Revelator. The thread can be followed through the centuries—through the diverse poetic visions of Dante, Bernard of Clairvaux, Donne, Herbert, Milton, Hopkins, Eliot, R. S. Thomas, and Denise Levertov—down to the poet whose work is in your hand. With the selection of this volume you are entering this enduring tradition, and as a reader contributing to it.

—D.S. Martin
Series Editor

Slender Warble

Poems

SUSAN COWGER

CASCADE *Books* • Eugene, Oregon

SLENDER WARBLE
Poems

The Poiema Poetry Series

Copyright © 2020 Susan Cowger. All rights reserved. Except for brief quotations in critical publications or reviews, no part of this book may be reproduced in any manner without prior written permission from the publisher. Write: Permissions, Wipf and Stock Publishers, 199 W. 8th Ave., Suite 3, Eugene, OR 97401.

Cascade Books
An Imprint of Wipf and Stock Publishers
199 W. 8th Ave., Suite 3
Eugene, OR 97401

www.wipfandstock.com

PAPERBACK ISBN: 978-1-7252-5167-0
HARDCOVER ISBN: 978-1-7252-5168-7
EBOOK ISBN: 978-1-7252-5169-4

Cataloguing-in-Publication data:

Names: Cowger, Susan, author.

Title: Slender warble : poems / Susan Cowger.

Description: Eugene, OR: Cascade Books, 2019 | The Poiema Poetry Series.

Identifiers: ISBN 978-1-7252-5167-0 (paperback). | ISBN 978-1-7252-5168-7 (hardcover). | ISBN 978-1-7252-5169-4 (ebook).

Subjects: LCSH: American poetry.

Classification: PS3603.O8887 S65 2020 (paperback) | PS3603.O8887 (ebook)

Manufactured in the U.S.A.   02/28/20

For Dana, my beloved,
for those who long for a word from God,
for Laurie Klein who hears the music and knows the words,

and above all for the One who is the Word

For of Him and through Him and to Him are all things . . .
(ROMANS 11:36)

Contents

A Note to You (a Preface)

A nose-to-nose encounter with God, would be blinding. Thankfully for now, God is invisible. Yet this too perplexes believers. Seemingly absent, his promised presence becomes, at times, a black hole into which prayers are shouted, a field of gravity so dense one wonders how love embodies the core.

Have you been there?

Mostly, we shrug and go back to life.

And perhaps that's how it begins, no more than a chirp filtering through the noise of life; a snatch of birdsong that makes you sit up, cock your head, and hasten to the window.

Perhaps, the song was not only made for you, it was sung to you. A small nudge from Him.

I tremble putting nudges into words. The presence of God reliably resists being pinned down. These pages explore universal humanness, challenges that break us, that save us. Through them may He himself elucidate the Warbler in ways you could not guess.

Susan Cowger

In the Tunnel

Weather Report

September 28   Dawn

Between seasons   I find bees
grounded on the porch
drones scattered abuloo
clear cellophane wings
spilled   stepped on   I climb
a ladder   scout for the hive
and the burden of sweetness
somewhere inside these walls

January

Elbow on the kitchen table
she cradles the orb in her palm
She says to him   *I am nothing*

He watches her catch on the wound
slide a thumb under the skin
and open the flesh

She strips the peel in one long strand
and curls the skin back
into a semblance of wholeness

slumpy and squat
She wrenches the pith apart
separates her life into segments

Even the sweetest juice
burns raw hangnails
She shoves the whole lot his direction

He arranges the fruit
picking up each slice
savoring   swallowing

They sit quietly touching hands
listening to time
the fathomless globe between them

She Memorized His Back

She memorized his back
her palms
rolling its entire Palouse
flush hills and amber fields
an undulation of worth

settled against tilted strata
the casual mention of neediness
an escarpment
thin as morning mist
around her shoulders
She breathes
against his neck

its reassuring smell
soap and sweat and all that needs water
the great thirst
no one lives without

Promise Remembered

He drove her up the old buffalo road
between the Bridger and Gallatin Mountains
and held her hand   They followed rails
into a tunnel quiet   so quiet
sound might have forgotten this passage

so they whispered   walking through the mountain
following an illusion of parallel lives
They only looked back   now and then
as the light came closer   a kind of star
forcing its way down the hole
pushing dank air out of the way
Wind bolted down the tracks
on a dead run ahead of the engine

What is it about a promise
that resolves to outrun a train
the black smell of creosote
and the scream of steel

on steel   He yanks her down
rolls her off the tracks   pushing her head
away from the tie   and deafening screech
Ba-bump   ba-bump ba-bump   the beating
and bleating coming hard   and hush

She remembers he is there
when his arms come down around her shoulders
and his hands loosen over her ears
an opening   so tender
she will never forget

Standing Her Ground

Reviewing arguments
she touches
the off-ebon of a bruise

and assures herself
it's good to stand firm when
you have a rock

a diamond faceted into
a million different faces
truth so faithful each reflects

me
and you
in mid-air

as if we don't know
the sky is falling
the ground closer than we'd thought

Paradox Apples

Dawn the next day
a talc of clay swirls with rising heat

A dust-devil's frenzy hovers   recovers
and genuflects

Clearing his throat   God
continues with his man

that ideal little clod   and his Oo-la la
rubbed in slip and wind

Imagine the courtship   you know   them sneaking off
and the eventual duck & cover   Eye-opening

the way God casually drops them off at the border
hardpan and apple seed fleshed out in new leather

he & she not knowing quite how to feel
anything but damned   the overripe taste of self

still on their lips with
all the answers

Accidental Psalm

She kicks off the eiderdown
rolls toward the far
side of the moon

a caesura
between worlds
holds its breath

Lying in the dark
she flops a foot once or twice
over the exact place

where holding-out   reverses
a muffled excuse
the shift   a flexure

like a key change
a glissando upward

and the lilt of letting go fills
the dead of night
Singing

Change the Color of Sky

It's black   but still Christmas at seventy-five
miles per hour   through Montana midnight
the small drag of *oh no* pulls the long hope
of home off an icy December road in a spray of gravel
a whirling wedge of light circling
the shriek no one heard   three thousand
pounds rasping rubber against sod   steel
crushed into clay   cheat grass and sage
rocks   ground   then floating   flying free
everything broken
against the power pole   foreheads and glass   ribs and time
the brittle spine of the guitar packed against
a trunk of epiphany   honey and jam   the wooly new scarf
and baby Jesus   that chunky steel coffee mug
flung forty-five feet out the back window   It's waking
upside down   voices and vertigo
unable to breathe or unstrap from dust and
the dangle of sparks and one   only one call
makes it through this black hole   someone shouting
shouting my name   searching for us with headlights
from the old road   Errant oxygen bites through
a chest wall   silencing the howl of a lung's
collapse   how many times *1   2   3 lift   again lift*
The mercy of being almost there   a palm on the face
in lieu of morphine   An airlift
they call it while crooning *soon   soon enough*
you're above the wreckage and weather
watching the slow motion of earth and
now   a gentle turn into the rising sun

A Bucket Goes to the Well Empty

She names God her *Sandstone*
scrapes the rock with her initials
legs a-dangle over the edge of rimrocks

Let her tip back a little more wine from the bottle
and nibble a crust to keep the world
from spinning   while she stands on her own

careful to not lock her knees   She thinks about breathing in
the vast Yellowstone Valley   Sacrifice Cliff and
the Crazy Mountains way over there   named after a whisper

dubious stories and hazy gossip about a vision quest or was it
a dream   cradling her good life   happiness bludgeoned
from her arms until it was her fault   Nowadays insanity

barely unsettles the horizon   And corny as it sounds
to say the blues of heaven can ring out an anthem
listen to the way her soprano-self croons

to the comfort of emptiness   The arms of a basin
encircle the lunacy with goodness
as if perfection has always been there to hold the flaws

Two Buff Birds

There they go
Birds all a-flap
like wizened sycamore leaves
giving in to the way the world tilts
and spins off a lousy season
You've seen it   the sudden freeze
of your best and favorite colors
Goodbye calling out
how tremendous is the fall
Yep   you're feeling it now
Creepy little chill in the air   a caveat
hidden in the turn   everyone gets the boot
Chin up now   that's the plan
Chuck anything
you're afraid to lose
Oh I know your shaky salvation's
all a flutter   Just look at those two dry old leaves
going for it   plumage wide open and flapping
as if life on earth can be anything
but going down

My Father Disappears

Canada geese circle the lake
and underscore the collapse of a sunset
Everything going down
a skirr of feathers   feet forward
pinions flare   fold and tuck
for the imminent running-waddle

Geese on the ground don't look up
They swivel toward movement
shadows and unexpected coyotes
Honking ensues   so much like family
when death approaches
All the flapping & noise signals

giving up every bit of blue sky
a lifetime of savings   And what was his home
no more than feathers
slipping through the invisible

The Great Missoula Flood

Wind without warning
hisses across the continent   a thunderous surge
shoves the Bitterroot Mountains   gains momentum
over granite peaks   You know how wind rips
water from clouds and storms down the Rockies
seizing a peaceful day at the lake   whipping
your perfect life into whitecaps
I'm talking about the nod & shrug of permanence
having no say about the cracks
zipping through the ice dam

Then oh holy heaven   a whole ocean of water
grinds down hundreds of miles
carving cobblestone into scabland
filling every void & fissure with mud
Montana to Portland   A cascade-like defeat fans out
and settles in every swale & ditch   as if God himself
decides to finally take a break   lingering like a reflection
waiting out the soak

and settling of the question of why
with weeds   Irreverent first comers
that take over   weave between sagebrush & rye
yarrow & cone flower   miles and eons
of eventual Palouse   that name that means lawn
of heaven   fertility that comes from
long-suffering & catastrophic endurance
Some call it survival by death

Yes think of all that died and
yet here we are
pondering
the immortality of seed

Notes from the First Job

Depth and darkness perfect a womb
Five cells of the heart begin to beat
and   wanted or not
a baby treads water
in you but is not you
Is held but not yet held

     They call it breaking water
     but water does not break
     it leaks like a rumor
     stretched and torn
     Slight turn of the head   shoulders   chest
     and a face slips free

The mouth opens
with one terrifying need
to breathe

And from that first sharp intake of air
you understand hunger
you will never not love

The Clouds and the Glory

The shock of God with us
awakens a throe

not unlike a baby
gasping from gusts

of wind in her face
We suffer for air

beg without breath
The silent wide-eyed scream

Do something
fails

under muffled shadows and
stillness   the smell of wool

a blanket thrown
over your head

And next to your ear
It's ok it's ok

Between Two Hands

Weather Report

June 30   Midafternoon

I have a rock I call the universe
palm-sized and somewhat flat

Here   press it between your hands
Warm the universe

What is it about smooth that makes you think
soft   Brush the expanse around your lips

where most of the nerves are
The universe is nothing at all

like flesh   wet the rock
The universe smells like rain

like a storm rising
between two hands

Gratitude's Shadow

Let's call it happiness   otherwise known as
the birdfeeder raid   Nimble squirrel
quickened by hostile dog out of nowhere   negotiates
a hasty arc straight up the oak's sudden vertical

Squirrel nests   no more than a snarl
of twig & leaf   fall
far short of a proper hidey-hole
with locks & alarms to discourage
avengers   but for him   today   it's enough height
to curl into another eventide

the fading refrain of life
taken up afresh by a coyote chorus   Riotous yips
jubilate over the fallen   A goose this time

Go ahead and imagine the feathery carnage
preceding that feast

Still I settle towards sleep   warmed with down comfort
Call it give & take   I lay awake   head on remnants of death
Someone's privation   my provision
And in the morning   every morning   I lift a louver
to find and accept what the sky offers

It's called wind hover   the beauty of a red-tailed hawk's
midair pause   Don't look away   Watch those wings gyrate
and collapse into dive   Talons extend

and fix on the crucial crush & grab
So it begins   life's surge upward
claws full of death
and my morning's happiness trailing blood

Go Ahead Do It

Dust and blue-sky   pause   for the autumnal signal
has been given

It's open season on wildlife roaming the countryside
Let's call this higher calling   *civilized*

killing   Who can understand this kind of power
the way a scope magnifies one second until the smooth

squeeze begins
against a trigger

brown eyes looking straight back through every lens
in my head   with not a fuss or scream   more like

an answer   *if you must*
then yes   and the remarkable dignity of no choice

It seemed like a choice

Damn wayward hairs blowing
across my pluck   hunter's safety passed

paid-for license pocketed   protocols followed
my rights place me

inside the barbed wire   Nudging the etiquette of stillness
after the report   dust ruffles

around the irretrievable   Gutting the trophy
dragging the warm buck and its crimson aurora

back to the truck   I wonder who else has looked into the grey
fog of lifeless eyes   trying to make sense of something

like permission
looking down from a cross

Things I Saw in Her House

She says
she can't stand the piano
the racket of past pleasures that are not that
anymore   An unbearable screech
is the very thought of winding up that stool

I'm talking the gradual crescendo
of chemo   Her daughter's   side-effects
something like a thin wire
tangling between their shoulders
yanking them to car   toilet   bed   cutting
every reassurance short
including the yip of her little dog   Don't let him out
that unlocked door   Who cares anymore
about strangers or longevity or that you used to think
sharp knives
made cooking precisely divine
all those choices left in the sink
useless against the troublesome
faucet of medicine and protocol's
excessive spray   They have it down so fine

It's not ok   but ok   she says kicking aside the scree
holding out with purpose   Did I say holding
No there is no holding on to anything except
the quiet riot of words from the surgeon

   Put things in order

That head-snap's out there   three years now

while the world goes happily on
silent about her screaming on the floor
and *Oh God   what can that mean*

   just wait it out   waitwaitwait   they say

   Oh wait   she's fine   for now

For now she says   it's not about light   the one she has
determined stays on
all night every night   In the gauze of dim thoughts
what-if plays tag with *confusion   Why*
mystifies and collects on the mirror
She towels it off in the morning   stares
into the eyes of faith
and wonders what exactly that means
now

David & Bathsheba

I am thinking about a boy
pulling wings off a dragonfly
first one   then another
dismantling beauty

as if flight could be disassembled
and the exquisite wonder taped or tied
back on like a cape or rocket

Glassine wings crack and drift
to the ground   nothing at all
like the pang of first lust

or the ache that hovers
just out of sight   murmuring
about leaving lesser beings
that do not scream
to die

A Cry Too Soft to Hear

O Lord   if forever is now
contained in this skin   I wonder

what will happen to the place I scraped raw
ragged furrows scabbing over the pain

the flesh injured beyond bruise
a cataclysm designed to draw you

into being
something like protector

savior of a wound I created
as if I could believe you would come and love

what I hate

Things Without Words

Sky reflected on the lake

a wave washing broken shells

what the earth does to buried things

that which the oboe plays   the sound

of a shadow stirring

the shift of a promise

the brine of your iris   the way regret

sees backward   deceit under a brow

a squint that quiverers   dust

closing an iron jaw

A Drop of Dew Asks for Heaven

Let's call goodness *frondescence*
bushes of fat frosted purple

sag beneath their weight
each globe   a perfect huckleberry

waiting for lips
pies and jams and browned-betties

cobbled desire spooned into pans or jars
sealed and stored

a kind of stockpile that sits back
late in the season

with one more plum picked out of the dust
and a closetful of guilt for fruit left on the ground

Oh I see you wanting
what I have

and that's the sticky-lipped rub
You

peering over the lines and crosses
of the picket fence   delineating yours

and mine   with the dark-eyed
hungry look of a curse

28

as if when I swing the gate wide
and give the whole garden to you

there will be such goodness
you won't even want an apple

Cannot Know   Until You Do

Looking back
it might have been that table
on the patio   there under the tree

or the linen serviette next to porcelain plates
There's a knife of course   just sitting there
bearing its own weight on the rim

nudging the apple
He'd always imagined the color red
to be filled with wealth

and danger   Eve
no question   got a piece of that
You might remember her knowing shrug

Probably happened just like that
call it a break from weeding
sharpening a dull day   paring off the tough skin

savoring enlightenment
with the question
Why not

Having the Last Word

I'm holding a thought in my mouth
I've got it slick and smooth   it's hard
in the middle   like a mint
Confident Lil' Sass called to me from the lint
lining my pocket   And who would have thought
this could be a win
cooling the tongue   revising the breath   I want to say
It's righteous   I mean I'm actually kind of proud to have
remembered it   Popped it in my mouth
like a dotted whole note   Listen
there it goes   humming its refreshing tune
even while you're talking   Did you know
things like this make me want to cry
Vapors of *élan vital* cloud my eyes
until I can barely breathe
This is winning
You and I both know
what it takes to come out
fine   OK   I've spit it out
There it is   by your shoe

I knew you wouldn't touch it

Rules of Engagement

You hold your hand in front of the dash vent for
warmth but roll down the window to get coffee from
the brown box that calls out *Good morning   How are
you*   sitting in the spitting rain with five-hundred-and-
forty-three miles to drive   bracing yourself for M's
death   You pause   and say   *Fine   I'm fine
Decaf tall extra hot no whip mocha* because those
are the rules of engagement   And the rules are OK
with pulling ahead as the box answers back *Four
ninety-nine* to your exhaust and they are fine with a
good *oh shit*   if you keep it inside the car and
smile without showing too many teeth when the perky
voice turns out to have brunette roots and must be
forgiven for not remembering that you were fine   but
because she has asked again   additional rules engage
and   okay   *it's stage four cancer* and there are no rules
for that   no chance at all   really   nothing but her
pressing a penny into your palm   *for luck*

River Styx

A reliable map   veins
crisscross her chest
like script   passages   entire chapters
no one reads
notes to herself begin with a nick   a cut
more than skin deep

A familiar burn quivers through
the hemorrhage of what to do
with this bloody hell

And there it is   her little self
watching
not exactly finishing it   more like
seeing someone almost like her in the mirror
but backwards   free
and flitting around the room
with something akin to
thankfulness

How Memory Works

-for MV

An awkward smile
shores up the last hour
wanting to do this right
even the embarrassing
notion to
      touch
      everything
      One last time
he watches his hand
brush damp wisps of hair
off Linda's forehead
Their eyes catch
on her wheeze   each
      ragged
      pause   another
      moment
to remember the entire volume
called *Long and Happy Marriage*
They hide
regret for all their chapters
left unwritten   The unknown
stares from her eyes   With and without him
her last breath
      slips
      away

And his life shivers to half
she flayed from him
breastbone to lung
sternum from self
except for an endless
        deathless
        recall
a magnificent blue spasm that
loops eternal   end without end
over and again
See how   fiercely
        gone
        presses on
the last tender scene
a gift both heavier
and lighter than Linda ever was

Embalming Sorrow

I. Given Tears

Pour warm water
in an empty bowl
Make a place
to wash the dead

What cannot be restored
sinks
in clouded water

Do you know live cells
torn from the dead   scream
Please don't leave

One must air-dry this trembling
twist & sling the lave   and as
the slough of prayers fly
back to the sky
birds arise from nowhere

II. Tears Dried

Her steady warm breath
had dissolved like wind at dusk

Washing pale feet in dark water
he prepares to endure   packing

the dory with fishing gear   bait
from the garden   the forced

hardship shoving him off to
God knows where   He slouches

into the transom   rocks
against the motion of forty days

forty nights
quiescent under the pall

No dove   no olive branch
no rainbow

Crumbs

Canada Geese arrive in broken lines
Crabby honks and a brogue of demands

trail the sunset angel in charge of
green pastures and still waters

Nosirree you don't say it   but you think
Give it a rest

and with the tip of a wing
the compass swings north

and a hundred pinions fan against gravity
hover then drop   the birds stumble

a final lurch before skulking around the park
where for at least for a night

the children's breadcrumbs
lead home

Black Hills Dust

Gathering oomph he shuffles
to the roadside lookout   scans
the vast shimmer of emerald & blue
sky facing up from the water
He shades his brow with a hand
stares beyond sun-splattered waves
ignoring verdant copses
edging the basalt cliffs   soldiering
one end of the lake
still solid   but silent
And squinting   the old man searches
ancient accomplishments of creation
for a few molecules he left there
something to gather in his hands
wipe off with his hanky
and entrust to us for safe keeping after he's gone
We came here every summer he says
His last attempt
to hand over the best
of earthly treasure

Doing What He Can from This Side

At ninety-three   he's out in the woods
minding the chalky ash of his wife   scattering
dust down the hillside with a coffee cup
After upending the box   he chucks it in the garage
and gets out a chain saw   revving to life
the obvious theology of path-cutting to the river

Despite the bad shoulder
afterlife dogmas are heaped into piles   branch by branch
and left until the weather is right to burn his pile of slash
She had loved long needles   Ponderosa pine mostly
amid shivers of diseased aspen   She'd insisted on
a blaze   rather than chemical cures

He guesses clear cutting is a conjugal balance
between heaven and earth
chronic tasks   all a kind of cancer that involves
mowing and whacking the umbrage
And wild fruit that comes to nothing
but a memory of devastatingly good jam

Port Orford: Requiem

Old Man rents a room one-hundred feet up a cliff
The staircase spirals to a bedroom
where he lays her picture next to the bed
and sleeps with the dog and stars and wind on the window

In the morning he is still glad
vacancy means room for a dog
They both know what this is about
sniffing down the old paths
marking spots in the usual way
Someone else doing the thinking for a while

At dinner he orders the fish-of-the-day
from the peely-paint dive
right there on the dock   Sunset & Salt
Driftwood   Fossils   A whole sand dollar

Things the ocean gave her   come back to him
as the chop & swell grieve the seabed
Barrel breakers roll every thought
into a stun of green just under the wake
light sweeping off the perfect crest
turbulence   subsides   with a roar

Is This Where He Cries

The Work Shop he called it
a place filled with agates & rock saws
polishers & tumblers   scribbled notes
pinned to a board   lapidary secrets
conjured from a wall of books
all the important parts underlined

Just sitting down there   eyeing
a raw sapphire   fished
from a bucket of gravel
gave momentum
to the endless whirl of machines
a life of turning
hard things in small circles
and someone always wanting something
to heal every hurt   The good doctor
sprinkles diamond dust on the wheel and
out of nothing   shine

Good thing   he says to the terrier
You're still a pretty good dog
He scratches around the collar
Nope   we're not dead yet
Closing the door
he creaks his way up the stairs
One more time emptying doubt from his pockets
pebbles of possibilities roll off the dresser
glimmers of faith just out of reach
too hard to pick up anymore

I Watched You Breathe

I watched you breathe all night
staring into the grey throb   I named
the artery in your neck
Harbinger   then *Hope Enduring*
for each long exhale and   O Sweet Jesus

the waiting   the hush   a standstill

And then your chest would rise   Again
I'd take another breath

     They say hearing is the last sense to go
     Words will retain a certain potency right to the end
     along with remnants   urgency   last appeals
     longing to get out   *I'm sorry*
     I love you   Love you   Did you hear me
     but you just laid there

I hope you were listening
when I whispered one last ask
for the road   something I imagined
you to do on the other side
as if some shred of belief
might up and wonder at some point
What the hell

Dear God   Can you believe I told him
to watch for You

Light Theory

Twilight fingers the ledge
and peers in the window

Rays flare a moment   and bend
through a water glass on the table

She takes a sip   sets the tumbler down
and watches light dandle between particle and wave

what feels like *Hello* and *Good-bye*
at the same time   Like the call

of a bird   the rapturous refrains
darken a persistent knock on the door

She stands in the half-light
afraid to choose

between what she loves and
who is calling her name

Bigger Than Him

Taller than he was
he named the smooth heartwood   *walking stick*

But for a three-year-old trying to be older
it's not about rambling   or running

being first down the trail   nor about the tangle
of want and need in his legs

and it's not about the way we roll
the pitiful scraping of a small chin

while the spine   backbends around
that roll and skiddish landing

It's not the interminable pause   the extended
yeow before there is   breath   or comforting coos

This is about the apple   in his other hand
the arching grace of fruit

bump and rolling to a stop
waiting   on the other side of the parking lot

a shiny sort of sweetness
brushed off and bitten into   after it's over

Confessions of the Deaf

No sighing in the night   No snores
The missing sounds of sleep
                    Oh there you are my love

silhouetted against the wall
The rhythmic rise and fall of the ages
                    and your face

dusky as the dark side of the moon
still remarkably full of planetshine
                    and small fissures

stories and mirth   we wish
were not quite so articulately
                    pressed into skin

Around the mouth and eyes
deeper revelations squint and frown
                    etch out love

in lines
so simple
                    a child can hear it

Is that you

Weather Report

November 24   Dusk

Night leaned around
the porch   eased into
an urgent tamp of desire

Smoke from the fall   lingered
like a kiss   Love defied gravity
the way dry leaves

trembled on branches
when the Savior's last gust
It is finished   gave permission

to reach for His face
tearing a halo
between us

Elan Vital

It's what happens when you grow up without trees
Your father brings a willow branch from Detroit
wedges it into a bucket of sand

and waits for a miracle
Caring for a tree in Montana is a form of prayer
Drag out the hose every day

and water for years and years until the wind
finally blows it down and Dad lets you
strip off the bark   damp and green

so you can lay hands on the rare white flesh
as if it were God   naked
and lying down   incarnate

Time Awaits Her Arrival

The wind thinks in dark blue   parting the curtains
in a single flutter   the way memory answers its own questions

with the smell of summer   a stirring so early that waking comes
to nothing more than distant crowing

a little mumble that slips into crescendo   She listens for the skyscape
to tweedle extravagance   birdsong threading skyward while

the tincture of blueness blushes   and life can be imagined as
worthy of dahlias   bigger-than-life blooms

swelling the shadows   where teeming green weeds begin to lean
against the house with something like thirst   Soon the donkey next
door

punctuates every hour's determined bray   Deadlines
the blabbermouths of time   crow-caw and gull-nag until

sure enough   the whole shebang pulls over mid-afternoon
in random bursts of heat and heart   Air-gulping words

storm back home   staring into the star-like effect of oncoming cars
A draft almost cups her face and hair

Who is it that waits by the door in the ash of the day
sifting the remains   Who is it that whispers

Darkness isn't about the day   but about
seeing your heart

Enigma of Unanswered Prayer

I.

    O Invisible Rock Face
from which all things trickle down
teardrop to torrent   the ocean
held in your palms   and me
falling into the deeps where
horror & thirst touch tongues
Yet on the bluest days
certain mountains float the horizon
To you I look up

II.

    O Great Missoula Flood
the ravage of pride advances
over a scabland of faults
Upheaval fossilized with the first lie
is remembered evermore
in a billion small deaths   Our hearts
still tackle basalt's impossible climb
straight up
the six sides of guilt

III.

    O Top of the World
look at me
searching for rocks to hold me down
when wind does not stop
I cry out   *O Stone live forever*

but what I really mean is
Please God be here
Let me hold you
in my hand

Faith Walks into the Ocean . . .

. . . to see what goes on inside a wave
eyeing fish whose names are schools
of vowels   testing the swell and spume

all tanned and barefoot   wading
against ancient boundaries   and
just that fast dropping into coral

and whatever the hell else
fills your nose and mouth
eyes closed and rolling

O God help   That's blood
thin as water
I thought

as Faith crawled out and said   Look
this could be bad
the blue-black glittery spine embedded

in your heel   The urchin
from Abaddon made it further
onto land than Faith did into the ocean

We sit on the sand and watch the wound
not sure what it means
but curious to see what the hurt knows

The Unknown Language

Sangre de Cristo   Cascades
Granite Peak to Sunlight Basin
the Bitterroots and Bighorns   mountains I call
my angels   towers of pomp and majesty
fawned over as if any one of them
gives a rip   Our imperial assumptions
always one-sided   I call it
Church of the Missing Door
where a piebald eaglet waits
for what has been killed to come to him

Seeds melted from resin's captivity
by fire   irresistibly grow and grow

I call yips   back to the coyote   and name the black bear
Muggins   hoping for that kind of an in
A charm or goosebump to signify
I'm with them   and we   are *we*
from one and the same mind
This sort of reckoning is easy until you try
to get anything from the silence   like if it's true
no one's talking
while all that goodness echoes off the breastbone

Narrow Road

I once had a parakeet   that stared
from the wire cage

and kept an eye on me
I couldn't teach that bird to whistle

or get him to sing the song
pacing around my head

Maybe you know the one
It's called *Home Sweet Home*

Oh I wondered every day about locks
and cages for flying things

I hung love on every wire and peg
dangled a mirror and all my best lockets   golden ovals

and hearts   each promise burst open
the teeny photos eventually blowing away

I have to tell you I finally unhinged the door
and let him out   I've heard it said

love has a shadow
like black birds in flight

Certain feathered things will take off with the song
and never look back

And a Knee Goes Down
—with a nod to E.H.

Oh Lord   Invisible
you seem not really there
Even though I want you
you hide   Sometimes I huck around
in hubris and hunger and swear
your nothingness touches me

and yet I get cold
lying on the grass
cloaked in cumulus
another forty-days-patience
counted in raindrops
waiting for what   I don't know

Please tell me what you see
is more than reeking seepage
my outerwear of despair
rotting the stitches
of shoe and sweater   Here I am
continually shaking the umbrella
of hope

picturing myself being laughed to scorn
for stupid questions like
why can't I sing   or have curly hair   win
why can't I win
or be the boss of you   just once
or know for certain your nothingness

delights in me

God as Water

Sometimes God is a pool
where the cheeky swimmer dares to lie
on the surface   buoyant

No one thinks a thing of it
when the Lord rivers a careful wader deeper
no footings   no holds

until the kick-scream choke of an innocent   falling in
concedes to rip-tide   Broken teeth
and ragged questions bleed from the scrapes

Wounds ground with coral and rocks swell oh the swells
When God is ocean
beauty and power breaks

every perfect shell
and shores its way into willful lungs until you know
God is flood

infinite   unbound   weight over my head
and the unanswerable question

Thirst

Hoodwinked

A hood keeps the long-wing calm
Darkness holds a hawk

Confined to a deficit   hunger pays attention
remembers tossed tidbits of steak

benevolences flung out of nowhere
like prayers   Small offerings

one chaw at a time
become something   code for

invisible tethers
threaded with an inclination to scream   Yes you do

screech and bate   It's the vocabulary of asking
for a little help here

and everyone's thinking
                    the bird's gone it's gone   but you're still

holding out your hand just so   to shade your eyes
when faith has flown farther than it's ever been

and waiting for an almost imperceptible   lift of chin
an ear turning toward   the slightest note   tiny bells

tied to tailfeathers
hope that can be followed   but not caught

A Shard Lodged Under a Rib

—Ephesians 2:22

      Dear God
I assume a lodging has been hollowed out
      for you
behind breastbone or lung
      a grotto
      where collarbones meet
      pointing toward
an ancient and forgotten chamber of the heart
      a haven for the Ghost himself
      My God
could it be
      a boat
      in all this blood
riding the torrent that moves to save
      tendon and gristle
      gliding   guiding the squall
of doubt and argument
      Where the two sides of my face leak vowels
      curdled and peevish
when I call to you and hear
      gibberish
      it's so hard to know
how you get around
      emptiness that is full
      of snot and pride
and you of all things
      comingling
      shame and . . .

The prayer ends here
Eyes flicker open
then close

To what can never be known
small ripples
dance down the spine

Giving Her Word

Finally   a sigh of distant morning
stretches out   insistent on more light
to frame the incessant churp
the exuberance of robin

rejoined by a million or so dirt-brown birds
and crowned by the sound of a quail's singular crow
his infantry scurrying bush to shrub
racing shadows across open ground

Sienna and gamboge spill out and spread
crepuscular rays   Oh don't get distracted
by rude jays   and the questionable brightness
of a donkey

Who on earth has a donkey
but there he is again   blurting a full-mouthed shaggy
heehaw   the way the smallest puddle
mirrors the shout of creation

and every wild instinct aligns to face the molten sun
Eternity   pauses   waits
as if there is no end
nothing more   than all

Still Not Sure

      Faith
is not the curtain of heaven
pulled back   It's more like reaching
back inside   having thrown *sorry* into all the holes
until those bright tears in the night sky have been utterly
      filled in
every misstep's erased into nothingness   And there you are
darkly waiting with a certain kind of pacing
hoping for a nudge or a wink
meaning *He's still here*   *but not here*   Kind of
like being told the secret to life
while promising
      to wait

Nascent

There is sobbing   bruises bloom
skin stretched until torn   New life pushed out
takes a breath   and I breathe you in

God   you arrived out of my darkness
How can it be that even at birth I could see
you in me

us gazing at each other
your fingers   knuckle and nail   a palm
and you grabbing my hand

Please name me *Endless Anthem*
the wordless lullaby
for incessant sucking

the way you and I
cannot stop or bear to leave
or quit or speak a suasive thing

to times gone by
as if anything could have existed
before knowing you

Night Calls the Day Father

Eve takes off to the field
where Adam's digging
to the other side of the world

a last chance she calls: The Big Hole
Not exactly a sure way to heaven   she says
Mostly it's endless

a reduction of dirt   and promise
that never arrives   Something like
the longest night

where sometime toward dawn
you crawl out
and lay on the sod

Same old dust keeps vigil over each breath
Light blushes the horizon one more time
as if it were the first day   and rising from the soil

a faint fragrance of green

The Way We Heal

The fading sun
cannot be called a fireball anymore
slipping behind clouds and horizon
Let's call it a dusky finger-printed window
letting in the evening colors I gather

into a quilt   lines of triangles
called flying geese
not even close to real migrations
where perfect patterns know where to go
for warmth   My need to piece

some kind of brilliance together
isn't what you might think   It's not
a cover   more like realizing He wears
a familiar hem   one
I might be able to touch

Almost Alive

Dun-colored little beast
skitters across the autumnal lawn
hunkers against a thistle   I'm squinting from the window
watching whatever-it-is bumble around out there

A li'l jump & giddy-up   then a mad dash
over open lawn   what is this
running for its life
Oh no   it's caught
stuck on something   nothing
Oh boy   I'm thinking   *this is it*

And now you are watching with me
another half an hour   both of us a-tremble
Yes we pray for an Almighty intervention
minutes sliced into imagined last breaths
Reluctant to move from the window

we find ourselves hoping
one of us will get tea
fear gradually losing interest on the chase
The life   the death   residual horror gradually
forms a kind of dry beauty

like hydrangea blossoms in September
finding a certain brittle stability
Each fragile blossom hangs on the other
until the whole kit & caboodle is torn loose
and gusted across the lawn   the wind
making dead things look almost alive

Drafting

It's the uphill-too-tired-to-even-fall-over place
you pedal to for prayer

I'm telling you it hurts getting there
and frankly it's not exactly an easy destination

so wherever you are seems like the best place
to hop off the bike and call it good   for goodness sake

but there's a niggle in the back of your mind
squinting at you and mouthing the words

Something's heading this way   Are you in or out
And of course   I know it's Glory or Gehenna

I'm thinking this is like Moses trapped in the desert
OK I know he wasn't exactly cycling through sand

but I always wonder about meeting God up on the mountain
and hearing the riddle of words

    Follow me
    and stay behind

Before I can beg a benediction
he's taken off straight down some narrow road

across the Palestinian Palouse   down on the drops
at a breakneck pace

and then just like God Almighty
he's upright with no hands

hollering   *Get closer*
inches away from the Utmost Wreck

Remember
we are talking about prayer now

and understand as long as this keeps up
there are no right words

just staying flat out at the end of myself
staring into the backside of light

where I am
filled with disbelief

at the lacuna
of stillness

From the Rimrocks Over Billings

 Florid clouds
 turn evening westward
A canon of vermillion flares
and burns magenta
Go ahead and say what you're thinking
 Oh God
 is that you
scorching the edge of everyone's page
in a scene so red
no one can look away
 Mirage
 or miracle blooming
through the dust and smoke   honestly
no one will turn to embrace the dimday behind them
It's okay if you weep
 for want of words
 There are no words here
It's really nothing   or the very last thing
the way we stare at gold
in reverence   waiting
 for something Almighty
 to speak

A Bird Tips Her Head Slightly

Summer was that cottage
far from noise and near to you
trying not to smile too much
Holding out an elbow   catching
cool air that eddies wherever you've been

and gone   No one knows how long
I'll wait   linger for days
south window open   doing my best
to lift light   into emptiness

where I've decided to stay
in the smell of pine
and dust   watching for migrations
birds like promises returning to us
with a slender warble

A Voice Clears

Weather Report August 17

Advisory   4 pm

Top lit thunder heads
O fearful breasts of heaven
Our mouths open wide

In a Strange Land

Before that

dust was nameless
Time sluiced around
a pool of murk
with no clue
to the shape of things
apples or heaven
What you call the fall
was more like drifting fog
a dim beginning that stretched out

an unsupervised hand

and was vaguely astonished
after eons of waiting for basalt
to shove its weight
underwater   Defying all odds
the granite crust bobbed to the side
like a cork
when continental plates collided

Let's call that bump a Kiss
something like Uh-Oh
as if the whole kibosh was
born for trouble   sparks
flying upward
morning and night
flipping over each other
and light   O Dear God

light running wild
color breaking all the rules
amid the warm eloquence of heat
Holy God you   command the fire
A jaw-dropping spectacle
nameless and virgin

After that I knew

I was not alone

Rapture

The osprey hovers
defying gravity

and a current quickens
between jaw and heart

This is not about belief
swimming in an ocean of doubt

or the astonishment
of talons   striking

being snatched out of nowhere
in a heave of wet wings

This is a fish flying
headfirst and into the wind

without feather or oeuvre
to save himself

Learning the Lord's Prayer

Come now your kingdom   please let it be
Montana or heaven   or something like
an icy lake above timberline
reflecting your face
        Is this what you're thinking
I'm thinking of the Pryor Mountains just there
along the horizon to the south   elongated blue
a little bluer than sky   I'm seeing heaven on earth
Manageable at a distance   but immovable
the way prayer feels like a promise
racing through prairie sage
the only place left where one can capture and keep
wild horses   Daddy said do it
        and it was ours
He didn't blink or snigger   though I imagine some mirth
in the power of yes
Yes   smack in the face of no way in hell
It was up to me   and it still feels that way
Like he wants it   Hopes I'll give it a go

The Meaning of Tame

Take a couple of feral horses   a stallion & mare
Soon a gangly foal drops into the dust
new life a free fall   quickened
with artless and lubberly
attempts to stand

All boots and jeans and been-there-before
closes the gate   moves in like he owns the place
touching   rubbing each hoof   Heaving the colt
on its side   he kneels   on the ribs and leans on the chest
with all his weight   covering the struggle   staying
right on top of him running hands
over the hills of pastern and fetlock
until sometime before   saddles   a nail is hammered
into the hoof   and it's not the end of the world

Imagine now an animal weighing more
than a ton   Listen to it nicker when he calls
and follow his whistle   Now watch him
climb up on all that weight   both of them
just a little afraid

I Painted a Little Bird

Pale as air
an empty canvas is nothing
but promises
I am grinding to powder
lapis lazuli   fine as talc
Oiled and stirred   ah blue
Sky   I see you now

My brush full of umber
clouds the updraft of azure
Don't get too excited
This is called   *Nothing Yet*
It's the almost-quitting place where

every mark
is an open mouth   a frown
busied with the happenstance of longing
a whole stratosphere taking on
the tone of awkward pleading
that becomes

a simple bird
a V
scrawled messily onto sail cloth
as if the very idea of wind
might possibly conceive

a gyre of flight
Almost a joke   Sort of
something   Just there
Kind of nothing

but soaring

Watch This

Let's call it a drop of water
hanging on a bare brown branch

You can use that one there
left by the sprinkler

or yesterday's drizzle
Please call it yours   for now

or forget the branch   just wait for the fall
It will fall

And that's it really   but don't worry
this is not just about gravity

or even the way ablution
slurs words of confession   though it is

hard to convey the weight of release
that winks of free fall

that brief but perfect sphere
of mirth   descending

Fast Water

Lie face down on the water
Stretch and pull   kick
Swimming has a ragged way of breathing

She coughs underwater   rolls
and sips air behind her own wake
Tuesdays and Fridays   there's a rhythm
to small obediences   Baptism
disguised as laps

and sharp turns
the downward roll and nasal burn
feet feeling for the wall then
surge and glide oh come surface   come
to the long and twisted lung
What is it about the deep end that makes you think
you can breathe   under water
testing the impossible in certain dreams
where slow   even   movement
allows the unthinkable
but the will resolutely panics and faith
bolts upright in bed   gasps

So many things about the pool
Claustrophobic ceilings   The dark current
along that one wall · and the unquenchable thirst
for fast water   the part of swimming
fish understand   the fastest water

laying right there on the surface   Like a reflection
Something otherworldly   A front crawl
turns into flying   it's heaven
so thin and parting   almost forbidden

Giving Up

In my story
those two were committed
one to another   right from the start
taking sniggers and rude imaginings
on as one   for a good nine months

So it must have seemed a little awkward
when she slumped in a stall
laboring to care at all

FINE   I'M GIVING UP

Now I'm sure you know words
even those words
aren't any kind of brake
on the orbit of stars
or ill-timed travail
creepy slit-eyed
goats and jackasses looking on
and honestly   the lowing

But listen   giving up
is the complete go ahead
for yelling off pain
Nope   now you don't even care that much
how long
long will be   not just
the donkey ride

but the extended and bloody
groan they call labor
with the promised stretch & tear

Come on Baby
Joseph says   *He's crowning*

And with that a perfect life slips free

Oh and then there's the knife
the cord between his fingers
In my story Mary lays a hand on Joseph's
to delay the inevitable
They watch the umbilical artery's
strong beat   abate
and soon enough   it is finished
Every last drop of shared blood
given up

Ablution

Brisk be the water at the pool
Best to jump in all-at-once
kickoffthewallandgiveitallyouvegot
until you feel warmer
    There it is again
the fast water near the surface
buoyant   nimbly laid out
And you   face down again
staring long   into the deeps
where it is hard to imagine
wanting or needing anything
      other than
a simple turn of the head

Dumbfounded

First   we couldn't help it
belief & doubt falling down
        afraid

of the roiling night   sky aflame
Stars enlarged   Constellations turning on edge
        and facing us   They looked right at us

in fierce shining flight   Those were wings
fanning our fields   a fearsome pulse of pinions
        thrumming

the song oh the song   such noise   an anthem
paean unspeakable
        pouring over us

We sang   belted out at the top of our lungs
the thunderous chorus   going on and on
        maybe for hours

right to the end   with that one note
held
        a prolonged sigh

like a rushing wind
saying   go   GO   follow the glory
        born in dirt & straw

find your every past & future
wrapped in a cloth and held by love
      sweet mother of God

We ran all the way   and didn't stop
humming that one part
      Oh don't let me forget

how the last syllable unfurled joy
goodness
      only God can pronounce

The Way God Paints

God chooses ultramarine
blue of course   Me   I'm burnt umber
that reddish-brown color   There we stand

braving the white and
deckled edge of a cotton page
smooth paper of the hand-made sort

God takes his big fat
squirrel-hair brush
mops clear water across every inch

The sheen settles and God
says *Go*   A blop of blue and
something like sky falls

seeps and spreads   fans
into my skyline   the place
where blue and brown bleed

into gray   Thunderheads
blossom between mine and Thine's
lines   I'm afraid it's too dark so I wipe it

with my hand as if that smudge
won't still look like rain's a-comin'
an imminent downpour

I daub burnt brown into the damp horizon
just to be clear there is one   a muddy
kind of transparency regarding

our differences   I confess
I've spoiled the scene   overworked the day
God just stands there   watches it dry

I'm thinking *oh for the love*
God you can use another color   something brilliant
like yellow ochre

or new gamboge   do some sun somewhere
and oh so slowly God dips his brush
into the blackest black

scribbles across the top
an audacious signature
like birds seen from afar

You have to stand back to see it
See   those birds are taking off
aloft and flying   whoa   they're actually flying

off the page   No no no this cannot be
but there you are   no there I am
borne along on their soaring wing

as light beyond color bursts
all joy
with fear and sorrow

The torrent   a bluish rain of tears
brushed away

by the palm of His hand

All Authority (the word: Perfect)

Just say that word and
ripeness comes a runnin'
the way a melt of chocolate
trumpets your taste buds
into Shangri-La

Pronounce those two syllables
and watch a superlative swagger up to *almost*
    No wait
        Listen
This word is the piccolo's lightning encouraging
timpani's thunder   all that pounding
while violins sigh like the thirsty
And then rain   You can feel it
hear it   smell it again
It's that good

Shout this word and
whoosh   all eternity arrives
everblooming
and deeper than deep   wider
than all the bluster   ocean shores can muster
It's more than a
      mad razzle dazzle
      the universe afire
This word is a kind of prayer
a presence   like God
standing there nodding at me

as if I could be that good
or catch it   put it on
or sing out the superlative high C   and hold it
until the whole world applauds

It's the word that means he is dying to do
        what we both know I can't

God's Favorite Place

She begins at the trailhead   there just over the edge
four and a half miles and twelve hundred feet down
Hellroaring Canyon   All clouds and vista   you better believe
the man who loves her insisted on new boots
Fear's anthem   dark and blue   hums about hope
almost clearly   above the mist rising
The rushing too-warm-for-June cataract urges
snow melt into a river   With arms wide
she jumps rock to crag
jacket pockets swinging with a few pebbles
of doubt   And that was that   a wobble & awkward arc
the upward glance before a sprawling splash
raw thawed might   assaulting flesh & boulders
billions of years   and brand-new boots pulling
her under   Ooh God   cold so cold
And the man who loves her races along the crag
watching only the water and her head   keeping her lips
in sight   Dear God   finally sitting in the shallows
of all that ever mattered   *You're saved you're saved*

Acts of God

Back to the wall   the dumb old piano suffers
more than one raucous child reaching up
sounding a random key   just to hear
Stop that racket right now   their hands
clapped to their mouths   and that warning alone
makes the piano watched   leaned against
Let's call it five of us standing beside it
a little joy humming in the back of the throat
on repeat   like a nursery rhyme
not monkey business
more like a recurring suspicion
all the hoo-hah is intended
to draw you in
Someone blurts
        make the piano sing
Father smiles
        pulls out the creaky stool

He winds the seat an inch higher
watches his fingers remember where to line up
The quiet room flickers with one note   then two
and a fierce rhapsody
        catches and burns a permanent scar into time
Who won't remember
the beige couch slumped in the living room
and small voices   stopped
as if God himself might now be

dropping notes   like pearls
perfect pitch descending
on them   the dissonance of outright defiance
resolved in grace
        catching their breath

They are quiet as fear
then begging

    Do it again

The Reason for Song

A gauzy curtain parts
Evening's breath eases through the window
It's an upper room   you can smell the
sea-salt bluster out there   fluttering
the edge where the sunset
stares down a persistent tide   The meal's
punctuated by noisy gull-ish shoves
called family   now crowding in
And whether you asked for it or not
the whole world is now looking
at your dirty feet
and theirs   It's a tricky play
when God Almighty points
not so much at the grime
but to the way you ought to be
Showered at least   as he puts it   Needing
a rinse   as if that makes sense
And then he goes ahead
gets out the towel & bowl   at ease
touching our dirt   us
gazing out the window
nothing to say   embarrassed
waiting for it to be over

His voice begins again   the way kindness
gives a sigh and quiet thanks for
floury victuals   And a bit of cabernet
serves life up to the gloom
in the room   He gives a benediction
a promise of long expected

currents and shore-shifts   He says this
is that   Already
I can almost hear him
humming   punctuating the drift
into the night   that's his voice
starting up a hymn   kind of upbeat
written in the range of calling forth
Creation   Not so loud as to scare you
just enough vibrato to enclose each note
with a ripple that will spread

A Curious Win

From what strange land did fire emerge
In the beginning   no one says a word

about light gone mad   Somewhere inside
an inferno bellows

The blast of singe brimstones heaven to one side
while the world cowers and waits it out

Tankers and hotshots take on faith
Reason empties a garden hose on the holocaust

Every war ends this way
evergreens skeletal

stripped of all   save a few ragged cones
held hostage by scorch

dropping their seed
fearlessly

Happiness Carried on Her Back

I hear your song so seldom
sweet little call so softly dissolved
roundest drop with a glistening fall

Plummet of waking alone in the night
murmur of wind and wings
curls of smoke and tenebrous calls

A slender thread swings in the dark
clapper of glass and a silver bell
Lo a great presence stirs

lifts its head   and nuzzles my neck
and lays its great crown back to slumber
where just out of sight and never in front
I feel you breathing forever

Soli Deo Gloria

Acknowledgments

For encouragement beyond words, I thank my family.

Many thanks to editor and fellow poet, D. S. Martin. It is humbling to be in such good hands.

I doff my cap to Tammy Turner for the infectious good-will that embodies her technical expertise.

I am grateful to the editors of the following journals and anthologies in which these poems first appeared, sometimes in different form.

Adanna Journal: "January"

Crux: "Happiness Carried on Her Back"

In a Strange Land: "Black Hills Dust"
    "God as Water"
    "From the Rimrocks Over Billings"
    "My Father Disappears"

Presence: "Go Ahead Do It"

Poems for Ephesians: "The Shard Lodged Under a Rib"

Reformed Journal: "Bigger than Him"
    "Having the Last Word"

Scarab Hiding*: "Change the Color of Sky"
    "Rules of Engagement"

The McGuffin: "Time Awaits Her Arrival"

The Windhover: "Learning the Lord's Prayer"

Wising Up Anthology on Joy: "The Unknown Language"
    "Watch This"

The following poems also appeared in *In a Strange Land* (Poiema/Cascade): "Change the Color of Sky," "Happiness Carried on Her Back," "January," "Learning the Lord's Prayer"

*Scarab Hiding (Finishing Line Press)—Susan Cowger's chapbook

The Poiema Poetry Series